𝔜ou, 𝔐aking it 𝔗hrough

Original Quotations for Encouragement and Self-Reliance

❖   ❖   ❖

Dr. S. V. M. Maharaj

You, Making it Through
Original Quotations for Encouragement and Self-Reliance

Manufactured in the United States of America, United Kingdom or Australia.

ISBN: 978-0-692-28951-8
Library of Congress Control Number: 2014915420

FOREWORD

IT is only words, it is true;
but it is the best thing that I have—
that I give to you.

❖   ❖   ❖

ABUNDANCE

DEPENDING on by what name we it call, everyone indeed can have it all.

❖   ❖   ❖

DESPITE how dirt poor on the earth we are, equally—the sun shines on us all from afar.

❖   ❖   ❖

THE finest, most valuable, most precious things on Earth are no things at all; but rich moments that are—free to be had by all.

❖   ❖   ❖

THE sun shines brightly everywhere, on everyone it falls; what is most important, therefore, is available—to us all.

❖   ❖   ❖

WANT nothing, and you will want for nothing.

WE can never be: too grateful, too content, too happy.

❖ ❖ ❖

YOU have abundance, and there is now nothing you lack; for remember: You came into this world with—not the clothes on your back!

ACCOMPLISHING

ALWAYS do what you can do, and it will be enough to make the difference for you.

❖　❖　❖

DO the best that you can do, then move on you.

❖　❖　❖

IN whatever we are doing, it is what we should expect; be it at the start or middle or end, it needs to go step by step.

❖　❖　❖

IT is better to go slow, and then to have won; than to go fast, but not have gotten the job done.

❖　❖　❖

IT may not work, no; but do it anyway, then if need be, another way go.

THAT our day is coming, on this we can depend; therefore, what we would like to accomplish—we need to do before the end.

❖ ❖ ❖

THE thing they all said was impossible to do, somehow—got it done you.

❖ ❖ ❖

WHEN we make it a priority, what we want—becomes a reality.

❖ ❖ ❖

YOUR work is important know it, though no quantitative measure may show it.

ACTION

RATHER than hope and wait and see, let us resolve to do and be.

❖   ❖   ❖

SOME other time we can hope for a better day; we have to sail this ship forward—right now, today.

❖   ❖   ❖

YOU, not them, made it through; therefore, it is for you, not them to do.

❖   ❖   ❖

YOUR next step you—can today do.

AGING

AFTER your many accomplishments at 50 years old, may you just be getting started with—contributing to the world.

❖ ❖ ❖

ALLOW not the years to harden your heart, for heaviness and joy—can only survive apart.

❖ ❖ ❖

AS we get more flawed on the outside, with deeper lines in our face; let us become more perfected on the inside, as in, growing in grace.

❖ ❖ ❖

AS you are growing older with time, you are getting more and more sublime.

❖ ❖ ❖

FOR a healthy and elastic and supple mind, whether we are 40, 50, 60 or 99: We need to be doing something—for the first time.

LET us create rich lives as we get older, lives that are warmer and never colder.

❖ ❖ ❖

MOST of it can be compensated for with exercise, in our body any decline; other than that, usually everything else—gets better with time.

❖ ❖ ❖

NO matter how old in years we art, we may forever stay young at heart.

❖ ❖ ❖

ONCE a year in the fall, we do get to turn back time.

❖ ❖ ❖

OUR potential energy need not decrease as we age, for the source of this fuel is spiritual; we have the power to shine brighter with the years—it only depends on the individual.

TEMPERATURE °F is a lot like age: 70 is not quite there, 80 is perfect, but 90 can be awful.

❖ ❖ ❖

WE can remain, regardless of how old, the most joyous in all the world.

❖ ❖ ❖

WE shrink as we get older they say; but no, it is that we grow; for further we see with each experience and day.

ANIMALS

AND the very best of luck, to all baby—bunnies and squirrels and ducks.

❖   ❖   ❖

DOGS and young children know best what is important to do, all they want is to—spend time with you.

❖   ❖   ❖

HOW could the simple tug of a fish on your line be such a thrill? Because for a moment our quest to be one with a wild animal—we are getting to fulfill.

❖   ❖   ❖

HOW is it that watching natural animals always seems to have a way, of lifting the trial and tension and turmoil from our day?

IT has been written that the animals are stupid brutes, and just meat; here to do with as we please, and for us to eat; but careful, like all those disadvantaged, they show who we are by: How we choose—to them treat.

❖　❖　❖

IT is certainly not me nor you; more self-reliant than the animals—no one—it is who.

❖　❖　❖

LIKE the whale makes its way through the water each day, may you through the world—make your way.

ATTITUDE

EVEN though it is dreary outside, we can always choose to decide, to be sunny and cheerful and joyous on the inside.

❖   ❖   ❖

EXPECT less, and expect to be more pleasantly surprised.

❖   ❖   ❖

IN making it through and having strength and fortitude, the first step is—having a positive attitude.

❖   ❖   ❖

LET us endeavor to because, we will make it through better, if we interacted with and dealt; with those that truly care and have a positive attitude and are happy to help.

THE ones with a poor attitude, are the same ones with a lack of gratitude.

❖   ❖   ❖

TO live in your life each minute with gratitude, is what it means, to have the right kind of attitude.

❖   ❖   ❖

WHEN we come with sure expectations, we will probably leave disappointed.

AUTHENTICITY

IN order to shine like the most brilliant star: You have—only to be who you are.

❖　❖　❖

PAINT or sing or write or whatever you do, always remember—it needs to ring true.

❖　❖　❖

REAL people are really happy.

❖　❖　❖

SOME animals walk with ostentatious pomp, others fly or swim with grand majesty; yet every moment is spent being—exactly as they were meant to be.

BEGINNINGS

JUST start to it do, and soon you will be it through.

❖ ❖ ❖

ONCE you have begun—you are nearly done.

❖ ❖ ❖

REGARDLESS of how big it is, to go no matter how far: You merely start—from where you are.

❖ ❖ ❖

THE most complicated break, to repair we can begin; and a new relationship make, by both agreeing to—simply start again.

❖ ❖ ❖

TO always have that special something, that love for life, that unquenchable thirst: Always keep learning or giving or creating something—that for you is a first.

WHEN it is what you had been putting off again and again, it is a great accomplishment to simply it begin.

❖   ❖   ❖

WITH every breath you get—another chance to do it yet.

❖   ❖   ❖

YOU can still make it through, because every moment—you can begin anew.

BEING A MAN

A failure as a man among men, is sure to be—a winner of a man.

❖   ❖   ❖

BEING a man, means of yourself having command.

❖   ❖   ❖

BEING a man, means take the heat you can.

❖   ❖   ❖

EVEN if in hunger and woe and want, and as a pauper you were reared; as successful as a prince you shall grow to be, and sporting a kingly beard.

❖   ❖   ❖

IF they were alive "no way" they would say, because our grandfathers would hardly it believe; that grown men hide and retreat and cower in the house today, because of from pollen—a cough and a sneeze!

BEING A MAN (cont.)

IT is not money and power that makes you a man; but the right attitude, a strong spirit, and doing— the best that you can.

❖   ❖   ❖

KNOW and keep what it means to be a man in your head, and this will better than anything else— stand you in good stead.

❖   ❖   ❖

SOMETHING to do, a little one or two, and a wife; is all that a simple and real and good man— would want out of life.

❖   ❖   ❖

STRENGTH has nothing to do, with brawn and muscle and sinew; but everything with you, being brave and honest and true.

BEING A MAN (cont.)

WHEN a wife and children you have got, but now the going has gotten tough; being a man means not turning your back on your lot, and showing of what—you are made of stuff.

❖　❖　❖

WHEN we are afraid to take a stand: We have forgotten—what it means to be a man.

❖　❖　❖

WOMEN can benefit from observing men: Instead of crying and complaining and all that din, for a man learns early—how to take it on the chin.

❖　❖　❖

YOU are from the do-it-yourself school, and a self-made man; you know how things work, can be counted on, and always—give it all you can.

BLESSINGS

ALWAYS very well by far, may it be that you are.

❖　❖　❖

IN all that you do, may all go very well for you.

❖　❖　❖

IT can keep us going, when we are going through strife and trouble and hell: A friend's photo, a stranger's smile, something from someone—who wishes us well.

❖　❖　❖

MAY my words caste around your life a spell: Protect you from harm, and in all endeavors—fare thee well.

❖　❖　❖

MAY you sleep soundly my sweet, until the sunshine adorns your bed and walls and sheet.

MAY your dreams lead the way, to where you are going today.

❖　❖　❖

WHEN we go out into the world, let us pray: That we return home in safety each day.

❖　❖　❖

WOULD that forever you—have good luck enough for two!

BODY

BECAUSE you are it in, love—every inch of your skin.

❖   ❖   ❖

CHANGES in our body, what is not right we know, and usually before any test or scan or result can it show.

❖   ❖   ❖

HELP your body help you, by daily what you choose to do.

❖   ❖   ❖

KNOW your body, baby: So your health is not a guessing game of—yes or no or maybe.

❖   ❖   ❖

SMOKING and overeating and not exercising are all forms of neglect, ways that we abuse and cheat and our own bodies disrespect.

BODY (cont.)

THE more we take care of our bodies in youth and middle age, the more likely our bodies will take care of us at a later stage.

❖　❖　❖

THROUGH your body from head down to toe, let good energy and lightness and love flow.

❖　❖　❖

WHETHER great agility and many talents or perhaps a deformity, our body is: The way that has for us the best utility.

BRAVERY

BE brave and strong, choose right not wrong.

❖ ❖ ❖

IT is hard to be a coward and truly succeed; the ones that are brave are the ones that lead.

❖ ❖ ❖

PERHAPS those not afraid to feel are less afraid to think; perhaps those not afraid to think are less afraid to act.

❖ ❖ ❖

THAT'S right—you coward, fight!

❖ ❖ ❖

THE moment we discover ourselves afraid, may the next second we find ourselves brave.

TO the problems in this world most prefer to turn their back; but let us be brave and face and tackle one or two, though the solutions we now lack.

❖   ❖   ❖

WE do not want weakness and fear—and what they bring—to become our lot; because it gets increasingly difficult to stand strong when: It was necessary to—but we had not.

❖   ❖   ❖

WHEN it is coming from a place that is good and true, there is nothing you need be afraid to do.

❖   ❖   ❖

WHEN we cannot the challenge defeat, nevertheless, it—we must meet.

CAREERS

80% of getting the job can be just showing up for the interview.

❖　❖　❖

MAY for you in your career, what is in store: Be all that you hope for—and more!

❖　❖　❖

NEVER mind who thinks you for the job unfit; a success you will be, just dig in with your will and grit.

❖　❖　❖

THE point in our job or work or career that we need to get to; is for nothing in the world, we would trade what we do.

❖　❖　❖

THERE is a lot at stake, so you have practiced what to say; look at it not as a dreaded job interview, but your—opportunity-to-shine-day.

CELEBRATION

A great big Happy Birthday wish, just for you: Congratulations on this many years making it through; may soon you reach a major goal, and in this life—may all your dreams come true!

❖   ❖   ❖

IT is not meant in a shallow way or like a boast, but because the best of everything you now have— a toast.

❖   ❖   ❖

LET us raise a glass in honor of you, for all that— you have come through.

❖   ❖   ❖

MAY your retirement be a wonderful celebration of you: A period when you finally get to do, what on this earth you were meant to; and that you are so busy, how you ever found time to go to work— who knew.

CONDUCT

BEING cross is not the way of the cross.

❖   ❖   ❖

FROM the rising of the sun, until the going down of the same; what matters most on this earth is: How another feels—upon hearing your name.

❖   ❖   ❖

I sleep very well at night due to the way, that I conduct myself during the day.

❖   ❖   ❖

REMEMBER to be generous, remember to be kind; remember that we should—always our manners mind.

❖   ❖   ❖

SAY nothing mean, but mean what you say; then saying what you mean, will win you the day.

CONDUCT (cont.)

THE inner differences in people are best viewed in how they outwardly deal with misfortune.

❖　❖　❖

THE way to live your dream and be content thee, is to conduct yourself like who—you always wanted to be.

❖　❖　❖

WHEN we do what is right and conduct ourselves so that our conscious is clear; we can walk into any room, and speak freely to anyone about anything, without fear.

CONTENTMENT

RATHER than always wanting more´ and to get ahead, we can choose to be happy with where we are instead.

❖ ❖ ❖

SO simple is my most indulgent dream: Saturday morning, the newspaper, and—coffee with heavy cream.

❖ ❖ ❖

STOP, and take a moment, and look around thee: That you already have what you are looking for— you will see.

❖ ❖ ❖

WANT everything—that you have only.

❖ ❖ ❖

WHEN we do what was meant, with where we are, we are content.

DEATH

AT the end of our matter, we want our lives to have mattered.

❖ ❖ ❖

LET us take a moment out of our lives to be moved by and know; that in any second, and in an instant—our lives can go.

❖ ❖ ❖

STAY strong and carry on, you can still make it better than just ok; because for your number being called—today is not the day!

❖ ❖ ❖

THAT one day our time on the earth will expire, we can depend; then it will be time for us to go to—a world without end.

DEATH (cont.)

THE purpose of life is simple, and nothing to make about a fuss: When we take our last breath, we would not want our lives to—have been about us.

❖   ❖   ❖

WHEN we pass on, what will matter is what we have passed on.

DECISIONS

LET us never forget as we live: The account that we will—one day have to give.

❖ ❖ ❖

THE big, overarching, powerful purpose of our life: Is to simply and quietly and humbly—choose what is right.

❖ ❖ ❖

THE decision that is always right, is never fueled by anger or pride or spite.

❖ ❖ ❖

THIS by now we all should know: Both by what we do—and choose not to—who we are we show.

❖ ❖ ❖

WHAT we do with our lives, including our careers, we all get to choose; and what we do about the setbacks, dictates in the long run, if we will win or lose.

DESTINY

BETTER we will make it through, when we do what we were born to do.

❖ ❖ ❖

OUR own great potential often we cannot foresee; continue working away, therefore, must you and me; so that we can become who—we were destined to be.

❖ ❖ ❖

THOUGH traveling the same road, let us not compare ourselves to one another; for we all have a different path from our sister or brother.

❖ ❖ ❖

WE must not fight destiny, what is written for us is bound to be; low let us bow before God's will, but always do what we can—while we have breath still.

WHERE we are, you and me, is: Always exactly—where we need to be.

❖ ❖ ❖

WHO we are choosing to be, is what will determine our destiny.

DISABILITY

AWAY from our one disability, let us; to our many abilities—refocus.

❖ ❖ ❖

BECAUSE of our more unfortunate condition of having no money or maybe a deformity, we can know greater about the world, better about society.

❖ ❖ ❖

BY carrying our burden, our cross, we are strengthened—from our loss.

❖ ❖ ❖

CAREFUL: It is our hate or anger or envy, which will most limit our capability.

❖ ❖ ❖

IT is hard to not conclude that life does stink, with so many things we cannot do; but "why me" we must never think, because our path—was intended for us to hew.

THEY all only choose to see, on the outside how we are bound by disability; but you and I know that we, on the inside are—light and graceful and free.

❖   ❖   ❖

THOUGH loss of energy in our limbs we may bemoan; all the while, in authentic power—we have grown.

❖   ❖   ❖

WE are all limited by our bodies, whether entirely able or fully not; the way to greater power is by tapping into the spirituality, each of us has got.

❖   ❖   ❖

WE would not be who we are today, since we shine more true and brighter; if it were not for the adversity that has come our way, which has made us a real fighter.

DISABILITY (cont.)

WHEN we cannot make it better for ourselves, maybe we were meant to—make it better for someone else.

❖ ❖ ❖

WITHIN an apparently agitated or flawed personality, or a distinctively disabled or disfigured body—rests a pure and perfect soul precisely.

DISASTER

FAR better me and you, will make it through; with analog and mechanical, than with digital and electrical; this is my notion, for like our muscles in motion; they can be counted on to be strong, to work and perform more long.

❖   ❖   ❖

I hate to have to it say: But when positive people are not optimistic about the future—trouble is on its way.

❖   ❖   ❖

IF the unfortunate is a must: May it happen to our finances, cars, home—anything but us.

❖   ❖   ❖

THAT we have to lose what we take for granted, let it be not; before we are grateful, for having it got.

WHEN all has been upended, it means you are on the up end—of it being ended.

❖   ❖   ❖

WHEN disaster strikes, it has a way; of reminding us of the gratefulness, we did mislay.

❖   ❖   ❖

WHEN the worst has come your way, it will not for long stay; and know that after the storm, it always dawns—a more brilliant new day.

DISEASE

A tumor inside us invades more and more as it grows; the longer we wait, surgery will be more invasive and more a matter of—who knows?

❖   ❖   ❖

CAUTION: Those cigarettes that you desire, smoking them is—playing with fire.

❖   ❖   ❖

IT is a dreadful and devastating and debilitating disease, I know; but all marvel at how the meaning of brave—to us you show.

❖   ❖   ❖

IT is like a monkey on your back: Smoking— weed or cigarettes or crack.

❖   ❖   ❖

IT is only the bravest among us that gets such an illness, you see; for it is to: Show the rest of us— how our future may be.

MEDICINE lies somewhere between science and art, and unfortunately for the patient—it is much closer to art.

❖　❖　❖

VISIT in the oncology section in a hospital one day, and to make you do all you can may, that be enough to—forever as a patient out stay.

DIVORCE

BECAUSE they found another, like the end of the world it may feel; but it is their false and dead-end world that they did themselves off in seal; while your future is alive with true possibilities—open and bright and real.

❖ ❖ ❖

CAREFUL: Married we can have it all, divided we are more likely to fall.

❖ ❖ ❖

IF he or she wanted to leave, no one could have made him or her stay; if he or she wanted to stay, no one could have taken him or her away.

DOING

BECAUSE never be able to do very much we would, does not mean that ever choose to do nothing we should.

❖ ❖ ❖

DO nothing, and there will be nothing doing.

❖ ❖ ❖

IN the time it takes to complain and blame, if we would but do it—we would be through it.

❖ ❖ ❖

SURELY do nothing, and nothing will surely come of it.

❖ ❖ ❖

WE have to do what we can do, even if that means only proposing a thing or two.

DYING

A better life from how it did begin, and when the time comes—the very best possible end.

❖   ❖   ❖

DYING and how incapacitating and bad the end of life can be, is a very good lesson for—anyone living to see.

❖   ❖   ❖

EVEN on our deathbed, and if we have taught others nothing before; we can show them how to die, to prepare them for—what is in store.

❖   ❖   ❖

LET us enjoy our little pleasures like looking at a painting or watching football while we live; for there might come a time, when in even eating our evening meal—no enjoyment does it give.

LIKE the sun, we can shine as we fall; and remember: When going down—the sun is most beautiful of all.

❖ ❖ ❖

MAY now that the end is near; we let go and embrace all, perhaps for the first time with no fear.

❖ ❖ ❖

SINCE we cannot accomplish much on the hospice bed, the time to get it done is—now, instead.

❖ ❖ ❖

THE greatest comfort on our deathbed: Is if about us "good," they will be able to have said.

EATING RIGHT

EVERY time we sit down to eat, it needs to be like some kind of unbelievable treat.

❖   ❖   ❖

GOD forbid, if we happen to not eat lunch or dinner one day; but guess what?—we will be more than ok.

❖   ❖   ❖

IF you are going to eat it, though you should not be: Count it out, and you will eat less, you will see.

❖   ❖   ❖

IT can start with a bad reason, like wanting to fit into that slinky dress; but end up being good, like now heavy, greasy foods you detest.

❖   ❖   ❖

JUST say no to junk food.

LADIES: Small and cute and little eat, is the way to get and stay petite.

❖   ❖   ❖

LET this not be where you are at: Saying that "it is not the food"—that is making you fat.

❖   ❖   ❖

NOT always does it mean you should eat when you feel that hunger within; instead, welcome and embrace it, because it means—you are getting thin.

❖   ❖   ❖

"SAVING room for dessert" means no longer being hungry—only after dessert.

❖   ❖   ❖

THE more we ate yesterday, the more we want to eat today; the less we eat today, the less we will need to eat the next day.

EATING RIGHT (cont.)

WE can all afford to eat less—and be better off for it.

❖   ❖   ❖

WITH this simple principle, it is a cinch to stay at a low weight: Only what is elegant is worth eating—in European portions on your plate.

❖   ❖   ❖

YOU know how, when we are really hungry, it tastes so good every morsel of food? That needs to be each day—at every meal—our level of gratitude.

ENCOURAGEMENT

A special gift from Nature for you, are sun-kissed orange roses and may; no matter what you are going through, they—lift your spirits and brighten your day.

❖   ❖   ❖

AS soon as you get into it, you will find that you can do it.

❖   ❖   ❖

IN due course you, of course, can it do.

❖   ❖   ❖

IN your search, you will come to see that I am not to you lying: Take that first step, keep going, and one day you will find—you are flying.

❖   ❖   ❖

IT is raining though, the sun is shining know.

ENCOURAGEMENT (cont.)

LET us continue continuing to encourage encouraging.

❖   ❖   ❖

WHAT we believe, is what we will achieve.

❖   ❖   ❖

WITH encouraging words, we get to give a priceless gift; as even the deepest sorrow that lay on another's heart—we may lift.

❖   ❖   ❖

YES, you—can do it, too!

EXERCISE

AS soon as we get going, the fat is going to go: going, going—gone.

❖　❖　❖

SHAPE up in one way, and you will shape up in another.

❖　❖　❖

THE less we exercise, the less we want, but more need to; the more we exercise, the more we want, but less need to, too.

❖　❖　❖

TRIM it down, and firm it up: arms, legs, belly, and butt.

❖　❖　❖

WE only need to, in order to be fit and trim: Value it enough—being healthy and thin.

WHEN we exercise, in our muscles, it is no ruse; we gain back ten-fold—the energy we use.

❖　❖　❖

WHEN you power your body, you empower your spirit.

❖　❖　❖

WORK your muscles, and your muscles will work for you.

FAILURE

BECAUSE of the failure and rejection, it is that we now know; in order to succeed, in what direction, is best for us to go.

❖   ❖   ❖

IF we have hands to throw up and declare it is to no avail, we have hands to keep trying—fail after fail.

❖   ❖   ❖

IT is about our attitude defeat; so it we will never meet—if we always stay upbeat.

❖   ❖   ❖

IT is ok that this time you did not make it through; for now, you know, what next you must do.

❖   ❖   ❖

LIKE every scientist knows, if it were not for getting it wrong and finding no smoking gun; to get the textbooks right—we would not have yet begun.

NATURE does not get or hold on to disappointment—but she does keep going.

❖ ❖ ❖

NO matter the number of times you fall, just make sure: That the number of times you get back up—is more.

❖ ❖ ❖

TO not let rejection get you down, never to the outcome be tied; because then, true happiness will reside; when, be it a success or failure, it just flows through you—so you can do what you are here to do.

❖ ❖ ❖

YES, of course, plan for success, but—have more plans for failure.

FASHION

DO what the universe has fashioned you for, and it is what will fit you best.

❖　❖　❖

FOR some, so hard is this life: For not one of her four pink leather dresses—fits just right.

❖　❖　❖

MAY the cloth that you are cut from be down to earth like cotton, but the fabric of your life be as rich as silk.

❖　❖　❖

THOSE that truly love fashion put in the effort, and make the sacrifices to be model-thin; because it takes away from the line and drape and design of the clothes, anything other than—bones and skin.

❖　❖　❖

WHEN you get skinny, with a skirt you can go mini.

FIGHT

HOLD on, pull yourself up, now you can struggle to your feet; know in your soul, all the while, in the end—you will not be beat.

❖ ❖ ❖

IT is an attempt to scare and bully and intimidate you, because work it just might; after your initial shock: Be sure to come back with a—good and hard and strong fight.

❖ ❖ ❖

IT is up to us, because each and every one of us can: Choose to cry like a baby, or—fight like a man.

❖ ❖ ❖

NEVER give in, and never give up righting; and if going down: Always—go down fighting.

FIGHT (cont.)

THE slightest bit of warmth and comfort, like a glimpse of the sun near the close of a cold and weary and trying day; can give us enough reprieve, to hope, and the energy we need—to fight on today.

❖　❖　❖

THE worst part is over, you have mustered up your fight; whatever happens now is—sure to be alright.

❖　❖　❖

THOSE that know they are in the wrong, cannot over time stand strong; those that are in the right, have deep within them—spark and passion and more fight.

❖　❖　❖

THOUGH eventually it will work out and be alright; when we are in the middle of it, our job is to—focus on the fight.

THOUGH it looks like it has been all said and done; as long as we keep fighting, there is still a chance—the day could be won.

❖　❖　❖

WE want it easy and smooth and to go without a hitch, because we do not want to have to fight; but the smallest bird chases away the largest—by simply being forthright.

❖　❖　❖

WHEN nobody is going to come and make it alright; when left is only you, still your duty to do, is to—stand your ground and fight.

❖　❖　❖

YES, they are going to try and grind your face into the ground; but whatever happens: Don't you—ever take it lying down!

YOU are young and strong and brave and bright, and so it is for you to what is bad fight; and save the next ones from getting over bowled, because they are—too poor or too weak or too sick or too old.

❖   ❖   ❖

YOU have been bent and beaten and broken, and yet, you will be ok; so long as you remember—never stop slugging away!

FOLLOWING THROUGH

IF you did not do it, but have should; you can go back now and do it, if you would.

❖ ❖ ❖

ONCE you have begun, follow through till you are done.

❖ ❖ ❖

YEAR to year or month to month or day to day, let us do something about what we—feel and think and say.

❖ ❖ ❖

YOU think that it is for another to do; because now, perhaps, it is too late for you; but no, it is your idea, and so—your duty to follow it through.

FORTITUDE

AFTER all the hardship that you have heard of and witnessed and personally gone through; when you see more troubles on the horizon—"let them come" say you.

❖　❖　❖

IF you cannot start strong—plod along; if you cannot carry on—drag on; if you cannot drag on—hold on.

❖　❖　❖

KEEP forging your way through, and you will emerge a—bigger and stronger and tougher you.

❖　❖　❖

MANY successful ones "made their own luck" as they prefer to say; but for those of us who never caught a break: To hew and forge and chisel through—is our only way.

FORTITUDE (cont.)

THROUGH your most terrible tribulation and trial, since you are still lucky enough to be on this earth—smile.

❖ ❖ ❖

WE need to forge on through the disappointment and disillusionment and all that is bad; because it often takes years to realize—what a blessing in disguise, we have had.

❖ ❖ ❖

WORTH more than a pot of gold, more in fact, than all the money in the world: Is your gained might, and your found strength—due to the fight, and from going the length.

❖ ❖ ❖

YOU have grown so strong from down to hell and back having gone, that now when a problem comes up, say—bring it on!

FRIENDSHIP

IF at one time you called each other friends, at any time you can always make amends.

❖ ❖ ❖

IT has great value and is amazing and powerful beyond measure: How friendship resides in our hearts—forever.

❖ ❖ ❖

REGARDLESS of what you are going through, your true friends will never abandon you.

❖ ❖ ❖

THE best person to be best friends with is no one else—but yourself.

❖ ❖ ❖

THE ones we have shared our hearts with, when we see them again; it always becomes—like no time it has been.

FRIENDSHIP (cont.)

THE roughest of road traveled with a friend, turns into an invigorating walk that we do not want to end.

❖   ❖   ❖

THOUGH old we can make friends that are new: By how we choose to act, and what we choose to do.

❖   ❖   ❖

WE do not know each other, our paths have not crossed; yet, we can look upon each other as— friends that have not met.

FUTURE

BUT most of the future is indeed ours to see: By what we are doing today, and who we are deciding to be.

❖ ❖ ❖

IF you knew what you will, when you are 80 know; in what direction would you now, tell yourself to go?

❖ ❖ ❖

IMAGINE if you knew way back then, where you would be now; that same difference awaits yet again, when one day you will look around, and say—"wow!"

❖ ❖ ❖

IT is onward and upward for you, and to better and brighter too.

IT is time to put the bitter days behind us, for recalling them makes us not constructive; together let us blaze on to our future of being—efficient and effective and productive.

❖ ❖ ❖

LET us hope that if not for us and today, that hope for another and the future—be there may.

❖ ❖ ❖

LET us not look down and back, but up and forward.

❖ ❖ ❖

MOVING toward your goals and dreams, this will keep you on track: Only to understand the present and go forward, look back; for example, what do you now need, because in the past, it was what you did lack?

THEY only saw what you were, what was then directly in front of their face; they never imagined what you could have become, not to mention— your jaw-dropping pace.

❖   ❖   ❖

TO get where you want to go, to what is holding you back—let go.

GIFTS

A gift is best when it includes something of ourselves.

❖ ❖ ❖

CAREFUL: To dally with the day, is to—throw the gift away.

❖ ❖ ❖

EVERYTHING that we have can be taken in an instant, and we can be left with not even a trace; therefore, what we have is not by our skill or smarts or strength, but all a gift given—by grace.

❖ ❖ ❖

THIS present that you received for free, time is ticking away on it for thee; God strikes the hour in the end, and will want to know: How did you—the gift spend?

GIFTS (cont.)

UPON waking, as if it were our last on Earth, is how we must treasure the day; for each is a precious gift, dear Heaven tailored and packaged and cared to send our way.

❖   ❖   ❖

WHEN each morning you rise, know there can be no greater gift or present or prize; when you return through that door, remember, nowhere else is something better for you in store; then when you close your eyes at night, the sweetest dreams will be yours until the morning light.

GIVING

IT just so happens that the reason we happen to have it, is in order to give it.

❖   ❖   ❖

LET us learn from living, and that it is ultimately not about getting—but giving.

❖   ❖   ❖

LET us not the gift treasure, but the giver remember.

❖   ❖   ❖

THE surest way to beyond your life live, is to what you never had—give.

❖   ❖   ❖

THOSE that do not live for themselves will never get bored of living; because they know there is always something more of themselves—that they can be giving.

WHILE we do and live, for it to have worth—we must give.

❖ ❖ ❖

WHILST most may look to get or take, let us seek to give or donate.

❖ ❖ ❖

WILL come to see, is important, me and you: Only what—for others we do.

GOALS

THIS is the goal to which we must strive: To live life consciously—and therefore—fully alive.

❖ ❖ ❖

TO accomplish our goals, though we often take them for granted, ultimately we are given only energy and time; may we use them wisely, and like all great gifts, we could not to them—ascribe a dime.

❖ ❖ ❖

TO find your life's goal, reach deep within your soul.

❖ ❖ ❖

TO serve our soul, must be our goal.

GOD

GOD always comes through; just not necessarily—in the way wanted, me and you.

❖   ❖   ❖

GOD is a she when it dwells in her; and a he when in him, it does occur.

❖   ❖   ❖

IN your deepest despair, one was always with you, always by your side; lovingly listening and silently supporting, since within you—he or she resides.

❖   ❖   ❖

SO few, God, so few—will past the test, and come back to you.

❖   ❖   ❖

TO make the most meaningful contributions and be effective at our job; that is, the best way to work is to be—an instrument of God.

GOD (cont.)

TRUST in God is not about—in hard times to doubt.

❖   ❖   ❖

WE can get very happy with ourselves, and it can be all so thrilling; but remember, there is never anything doing without—God willing.

❖   ❖   ❖

YOU know how, there has never been an atheist on a sinking ship? Well, just so, for that win or goal or success we want, we must not think we are owed or deserve or have even earned it, but be praying on our knees; down and low and true and meek and humble, as in: Please, God—please.

GRATITUDE

ACQUIRE the gift of gratitude in your heart, and presents you will forever find—in the midst of you art.

❖　❖　❖

BE so delighted upon waking each day, because this means—you get another say.

❖　❖　❖

EVEN if we are unlucky and depressed and poor, what we have to be grateful for is always—so much more.

❖　❖　❖

GREATFULDAY (a combination of "great" and "grateful" and "day") needs to be another weekend day; one that we can all use—in between Saturday and Sunday.

GRATITUDE (cont.)

LET it be that it is only the folly of youth that does not know what he or she has got; let it be that we—no matter what—give thanks for our lot.

❖ ❖ ❖

LET us appreciate anything anyone for us cares to do; because no one has to do anything, for me nor you.

❖ ❖ ❖

LET us be grateful for the kindnesses that we have received along the way; and the part in our lives for good—that chance has gotten to play.

❖ ❖ ❖

LET us be thankful for every moment of life, and equally in that moment if—joy or woe is rife.

LET us each morning when we wake, be grateful if to our beds again we it make; let us each day we leave our homes own, rejoice if we did not forever leave our loved ones alone; and let us when we go to bed each night, celebrate each day, upon seeing the morning light.

❖ ❖ ❖

LET us pause full of a grateful heart: For all that we have, and for where we art.

❖ ❖ ❖

MAY your tears of gratefulness for the grace and generosity and all you have received; wash away the grief and hurt and harm, and how you were deceived.

❖ ❖ ❖

THE best kind of attitude, is one of gratitude.

THE more gratitude in our heart, the more happy and content and at peace with ourselves we art.

❖ ❖ ❖

THE ones that are ecstatically grateful simply to be on the earth alive, are the ones in this world—who will always thrive.

❖ ❖ ❖

THIS is the level of appreciativeness to which we must strive: To be grateful beyond words—just to be alive.

❖ ❖ ❖

WAKE simply filled with the spirit of gratefulness, and happy to greet the day; and satisfaction of your deepest thirst and hunger, you will meet in every way.

GRIEVING

OUR lives need not be shattered, even if death takes the only one whom to us has ever mattered.

❖ ❖ ❖

THEIR time on the earth came to an end, but that they are at ease and peace, you can depend.

❖ ❖ ❖

WHEN a spouse dies, we can become whole again and stay afloat; because by now we are more like an—old and tough, chicken or goat.

❖ ❖ ❖

WHEN our loved ones do ultimately go, they become angels that guide us, know.

❖ ❖ ❖

WHEN the day has come, "death do you part," though you have been as one, lose not heart; you have grown strong independently, and alone can make your way now—even contentedly.

WHEN the ones we loved dearly are gone, for the ones that love us dearly—we need to carry on.

❖   ❖   ❖

WHEN we find ourselves dwelling on death, remember instead; that life is for the living, and death is for the dead.

❖   ❖   ❖

YOU were always better able to cope than he or she; so better in the end to struggle on by yourself—that it be thee.

GROWTH

DUE to our pride, or maybe being too cowardly inside, we did not say "thank you" or even allow our gratitude to show; but because of what they were brave enough to say, it made us better, we know; yet, now all can still be well, so long as from it—we grow.

❖　❖　❖

IN the midst of our trials and tribulations, if only at the time we knew; that we would one day look back astonished, at how much—from it we grew.

❖　❖　❖

WHEN a major problem in the day, or all the little difficulties along our way, leave us depleted; it will be ok, know, that it is for us to grow, up until we are—strong and whole and completed.

❖　❖　❖

WHEN we are depressed and in the deepest depths of low; when we are down and out, and to give in about, at the time we anything but this know: That each time we get back up—we grow.

HAPPINESS

BEING happy is as easy as 1-2-3; for it follows from being grateful—automatically.

❖ ❖ ❖

IF happiness we measured like we do gold, the poorest among us would have riches untold.

❖ ❖ ❖

MAY in your pursuit of happiness what you do—leads yourself back to you.

❖ ❖ ❖

THE more we have a grateful heart, the less likely we are to be unhappy about where we art.

❖ ❖ ❖

THE "pursuit of happiness" begins and ends with being grateful.

HAPPINESS (cont.)

THERE should be no "pursuit of happiness," our founding fathers got it completely wrong; it is not something to seek externally, but comes from within—and from being strong.

❖   ❖   ❖

WHEN one always does what is right, one is always happy—come what might.

❖   ❖   ❖

WHEN we bring warmth and love wherever we go, happiness and contentment we will truly know.

HARD WORK

HAVE faith and hope and pray, but always while you—keep plugging away.

❖ ❖ ❖

HEALTHY and wealthy you will be one day, because you are trying and plying today.

❖ ❖ ❖

IT was bound to be dear-bought, but your mind you had set-to; sure enough, it was hard-got, and shows—there is nothing you cannot do.

❖ ❖ ❖

OTHERS think it has been your good luck; you know it is your—grit and will and pluck.

❖ ❖ ❖

RATHER than covet that chancy or fleeting or unlikely prize or honor or award; know that doing the actual work is, in fact, the best and truest and most enriching reward.

HARD WORK (cont.)

THERE is great spirituality in hard work.

❖　❖　❖

WE are given the means and freedom and liberty, I will wager to bet: In order to choose—discipline and hard work and to toil and to sweat.

❖　❖　❖

WE sleep much better, when at night we lay our heads down to rest; when in the day—we gave our best.

❖　❖　❖

WORK, and it will work out well.

HEALTH

FOR weighing health benefits and risks, for us to by abide: Do everything to protect your health, and nothing to risk it—is an easy guide.

❖   ❖   ❖

IN order to get and stay healthy and strong and fit, with eating right and exercising—we have to never quit.

❖   ❖   ❖

LET us do all we can to protect our health, and may it be that we can then depend: On a life beautifully lived, where we are healthy to the end.

❖   ❖   ❖

LET us endeavor to change our fate, and not wait until we are in a poor state; before we value it enough, what we have at this date; because here is the thing with health: It can reach a point when—it gets too late.

LET us make it a priority, as without our health nothing gets done—nothing for nobody.

❖   ❖   ❖

LET us not wait until we have it not; if we are walking and talking, know that—everything we have got.

❖   ❖   ❖

MAYBE it is serious, or maybe it is nothing; but because we do not know, that is why off to the doctor we must go.

❖   ❖   ❖

SUBSCRIBING to the best health plan, means to protect it doing all you can.

❖   ❖   ❖

THE best type of health insurance is eating right, plus exercising and sleeping well at night.

THE thing we should actually love best to do: Is to get trim and firm and healthy, as this will—better get us through.

❖   ❖   ❖

WHETHER it is about health or something else that impacts me and you; many times, more than genetics or the environment that we are subject to; effects are determined largely based on—what about it we choose to do.

HELPING

BE someone you, that sees someone else through.

❖   ❖   ❖

IT can cost us nothing, to help another along, yet can save him or her everything—lending support strong.

❖   ❖   ❖

LET us make it a plan, to help the next person whenever and wherever we can.

❖   ❖   ❖

MOST worthy of our aid and help and a hand up, this is who: The ones with little money or means, yet trying with all they have got—to make it through.

❖   ❖   ❖

ONE of the reasons we have made it through, is to help others likewise do.

PERHAPS, the ones on their own who can survive, with just a little help would be able to thrive.

❖ ❖ ❖

WHEN you know what it is like, because it has happened to you; may to: Make it better for the next person be—what you decide to do.

❖ ❖ ❖

YOU cannot be helpless, when you are being helpful.

HOLIDAYS

AS we begin anew, another year: All my very best wishes to you, my dear.

❖   ❖   ❖

HEALTHY New Year!

❖   ❖   ❖

HOW much more beautiful is our Sunday, when we do not have to go to work on Monday?!

❖   ❖   ❖

IT is what I find most charming about this time of year: To send a holiday card—to let you know I care.

❖   ❖   ❖

LET us be joyous and grateful and cheer, to all—happy holidays and happy New Year!

MAY this New Year, you—meet with success in all you do.

❖ ❖ ❖

MUCH more relaxing is our Saturday, when we were off from work on Friday.

❖ ❖ ❖

WE get a fresh start with each New Year: To set all things right, to see more clear.

❖ ❖ ❖

WHETHER at home or away: May joy and love and health—be yours, this holiday.

HOME

As a child, feeling in your heart the love of your family at home; becomes a soft place to fall back on—anywhere when grown.

❖   ❖   ❖

In what makes a house into a home, we must include: home cooking and home-made food.

❖   ❖   ❖

Just like no one can hold a candle to your spouse; there is no "comparable" if it is what you love, like your house.

❖   ❖   ❖

The first condition in living peacefully, is that our living conditions include a peaceful home.

❖   ❖   ❖

The ultimate vacation spot to relax and roam: Is on one's own land, and in one's own home.

THROUGH our many years as husband and wife together, we shall live until our forever; in love and peace and joy beyond all telling—in our home, our humble dwelling.

❖ ❖ ❖

UNTO our home, this precious place; resides: love and happiness, and peace and grace.

❖ ❖ ❖

WE all need a home, that we want to come home to.

❖ ❖ ❖

WE can turn here into heaven, by making our home a happy haven.

❖ ❖ ❖

WE must not mind them, because they are not doing it out of lust; the wood logs in the fireplace—whistling at us.

WHEN love and contentment our hearts grace, always will our home be a happy and peaceful place.

❖ ❖ ❖

WHEN you share a recipe, you share your home.

❖ ❖ ❖

YOU have experienced luck greater than anything known, if "the one"—is waiting for you at home.

HONOR

EACH and every one of us would stand most tall, if we make our way the honorable way—or no way at all.

❖ ❖ ❖

IF we have no money or power or means, and of what we have left, it is all; we would be richer than what the kings of old have seen—when honor it is called.

❖ ❖ ❖

IT is wrong and unfair and backwards, but do not whine or cry or shout; to prove yourself worthy of respect and esteem and distinction—is what these trials are about.

❖ ❖ ❖

OUR acts and deeds and efforts, like the sun's rays; go on and do immeasurable good, when they are—honorable and brave.

WE do not want to be like a fool or joker or yo-yo; but sure and strong and honorable, so: Get it straight, and say it once—your "yes" or "no."

❖ ❖ ❖

WE would want to have done it honorably, not just to have made it through; but this tougher path becomes easy, when we choose to be—good and honest and true.

❖ ❖ ❖

WHEN honor or truth is at stake, when looking back that we chose; we will never regret that: We stood up—and took the blows.

HOPE

ABOVE and behind and beyond the blackest clouds on the greyest day: Remember that—the sun is still shining away.

❖ ❖ ❖

IT goes on this earth an astronomically long way: A little bit of from the sun—a ray.

❖ ❖ ❖

IT is a quality that is very special, because it keeps us trying, hope within; it is what is needed and essential—to stay in the game in order to win.

❖ ❖ ❖

MAY we find the hope in hopelessness.

❖ ❖ ❖

ON the darkest day with the deepest gloom and the heaviest clouds above; from where we are, we cannot see it, but the sun—is smiling brilliantly on us, with love.

REGARDLESS of how low we sink, even if on the ground we lie, we can always—look up at the sky.

❖   ❖   ❖

UNDER winter's ice and snow that is hard and cold and wet, lie all of summer's gentle tulips and irises and peonies—never forget.

❖   ❖   ❖

WE can never be truly poor, because we always have something we can hope for.

HUMBLENESS

CAREFUL: Those less humble, are much more likely to stumble.

❖ ❖ ❖

HE had worked hard since a lad, and deserved all he had, anyone would have said; but when asked about his life, that he has "been very lucky"—is what he did say instead.

❖ ❖ ❖

HUMBLER is always wiser.

❖ ❖ ❖

LET us value the awards and honors and riches of the world as indifferently, as our gifts and traits and abilities came to be genetically.

No matter our means or money, despite our position or title, regardless of our degrees or what we know; if we are human and alive on the earth, let us be wise enough to, in everything we do: With the utmost of humbleness—come and go.

❖   ❖   ❖

The poorer in ego we are, the better off by far.

❖   ❖   ❖

We all have sage lessons to learn yet; for example: The longer we live—the humbler we should get.

INDIVIDUALITY

AT times of course, their jeers and taunts sting; but whether you cry or shrug it off, just keep— doing your own thing.

❖   ❖   ❖

BE generous in your interpretation of what others do; be above letting anybody get your goat; give your love to only those who appreciate you for you; and never let anyone else—steer your boat.

❖   ❖   ❖

BECAUSE we can never be better than they are at being themselves, when we try to be like others, we are bound to fail; but when we are true, and put ourselves into what we do, we are certain to prevail.

❖   ❖   ❖

IN all the world, there has never been an example of you; therefore, the surest way to succeed is to— your own ideas pursue.

No, do not have to act we—like who they think we should be.

❖   ❖   ❖

ONE person can make a difference all else above; it depends singularly on what—he or she is made of.

❖   ❖   ❖

THE doctor and lawyer and politician today by their own choice, too afraid to speak their mind art; whereas, it is the poet and artist and writer that continue to voice, bravely—what is in their heart.

❖   ❖   ❖

THOUGH where we end up usually can be predicted based on where we start, quite common it is that promising ones by the wayside depart; so that we should never mind, but instead know we must be: Our own unique selves, especially—when we began behind.

TOO much, too many others, we mind; be your own special self: Be a—one-of-a-kind.

❖ ❖ ❖

WE are at our best, when we like Nature be: pure and authentic and original and free.

❖ ❖ ❖

WHEN we do not follow the crowd, we stand out from the crowd; and to stand out from the crowd we need, in order to—the crowd lead.

❖ ❖ ❖

WHEN you do not fit in, when there is no spot for you; it means: You will stand out as authentic and independent and original—in everything you choose to do.

❖ ❖ ❖

YOU are doing it right, when in what you do— who you are comes through.

JOY

FOR terrific fun and great stress relief: Simply try to—catch a falling leaf.

❖   ❖   ❖

FOR two days in a row, you would not believe what I did see: Going to eat mulberries and completely unaware of me; a grey fox went out of its way, to jump—for joy and fun and play— through a split-trunk tree!

❖   ❖   ❖

HOW the young deer in spring, romp and dance and all but sing; up and down the fields so fast, and round and round the rocks they go; what else is it but—the joy of living they show.

❖   ❖   ❖

IF only we had known then, the joy, of being—a little girl or boy.

LET us enjoy every day like a dream, like on the icing—whipped cream.

❖　❖　❖

MAY to look above and see, a maple in autumn all aglow; is what joy is to thee, and what it is—to heaven know.

❖　❖　❖

THERE are no moments that have greater worth, than a gathering where there is much—love and joy and mirth.

KINDNESS

KEEP in your mind, do what is kind.

❖   ❖   ❖

LET us spare a thought for those that are in need, and be ready with a kind—smile or word or deed.

❖   ❖   ❖

MAY with our hands, we act with our hearts.

❖   ❖   ❖

OF all the ways to be kind, the best is to give of your time.

❖   ❖   ❖

THAT hugs and kisses if you happen to foresee, are not appropriate to give to he or she, kind words and smiles—always will be.

❖   ❖   ❖

THERE are many kinds of kindness.

WE may think on a mean or bitter or angry day, that no one has cared to help us along the way; but how our lives would have gone without the little kindnesses—many unknown—we would not want to say.

❖   ❖   ❖

WHEN you do not know what to buy to give, know that a kind word will—anything material outlive.

LAND

IF you are for development, you are against Nature.

❖ ❖ ❖

THE greatest wealth as far as I can see, is to be rich in—blades of grass and flower and tree.

❖ ❖ ❖

WALK about the fields in stubble, and soon you will forget all your trouble.

❖ ❖ ❖

WE will never know anything more grand, than being out in the country, on the land.

❖ ❖ ❖

WHAT a beautiful thing, a coarse and scarred and calloused hand; when it comes from the hard and tough, but fine labor of—working on the land.

WHAT an extraordinary joy and pleasure, it is as if it were a dream: To come in from working out on the land, and simply—bathe and put on clothes clean.

❖   ❖   ❖

WHEN we are out on the land alone, we are accompanied by many a—bird and tree and stone.

LAUGHTER

IT is too much to handle, too much to deal with, because it is all too grave; but when we realize it has served us, it becomes all too funny, and comes about—because we forgave.

❖ ❖ ❖

NOTHING says "no class," like a tattoo—on your ass!

❖ ❖ ❖

THE best way to shrug it off, is to laugh it off.

❖ ❖ ❖

THOUGH indeed serious is the work that you do, still may your sense of humor come through.

❖ ❖ ❖

WE can be serious about being funny, and we can be funny about being serious.

LAUGHTER (cont.)

WHEN the problem will not go away, despite what you do: Laugh about it, and you may be surprised to find—it gets you through.

❖　❖　❖

WHEN you cannot help but frown, let someone else's laughter lift you from feeling down.

LEARNING

AVAILABLE in this one life, for each and every one of us to know: Is everything we need to fully learn and expand and grow.

❖ ❖ ❖

I know how it has been, I know what it is like, but there is no reason still, to cry or complain or shout; because: Your dreams and education and will, shall always be—the ticket out.

❖ ❖ ❖

IF after the situation you try and grow, then you learned what you needed to know.

❖ ❖ ❖

WHEN we look upon everything as an education for which we yearn, we will see that from anything, anywhere—we can always learn.

LIFE

HERE is a profound question, that to your life has value untold: How are you choosing here—to reveal your soul?

❖   ❖   ❖

IT is never about the cards we have been dealt, because—isn't that just the beginning of the game? Everything is open to us in the playing: happiness, love, wealth, and acclaim.

❖   ❖   ❖

JUST as it is wisest to always give the devil his due; for the parts in our lives they play, chance and luck and happenstance—we must never pooh-pooh.

❖   ❖   ❖

LIFE is not about the cards dealt, per se; but our hand has, indeed, been submitted to us to play; it is about what we choose and how we overcome the obstacles in our way; and when done right, as intended, we grow more powerful, like the heavenly body that dawns each day.

LIFE (cont.)

LIFE is often bittersweet; which means, if the first part was bitter, the rest will be like a confectioner's treat.

❖   ❖   ❖

LIFE was not meant for us to demand of it, but for us to meet its demands.

❖   ❖   ❖

YOUR little life each day—love in a big way!

LOOKS

A little vanity can be good, like when it keeps our weight where it be should.

❖   ❖   ❖

BEING truly confident comes from being comfortable in your skin; knowing who you are is the best type of beauty, the kind that—comes from within.

❖   ❖   ❖

IT costs not a single penny, imagine that: To look younger and taller and more beautiful, simply—lose the fat.

❖   ❖   ❖

REMEMBER that in all this wide world, anyone or anything rarely, that glitters is of gold; and often it is who or what that barely, catches our eye has value untold.

THE one to whom to give your heart, is who thinks you are beautiful—no matter how you art.

❖ ❖ ❖

TO look elegant, only eat what is elegant.

❖ ❖ ❖

WHEN we put our health before beauty, beauty will automatically follow.

LOSING WEIGHT

AN attitude of gratefulness alone can empower us to lose any amount of weight: To nothing but water are we entitled, and for every morsel of food, we must—give thanks and savor and celebrate.

❖ ❖ ❖

HAVE you tried all the little tricks to lose weight: Like having your dinner, instead, on a salad plate?

❖ ❖ ❖

HOW to lose weight? Why it could not be a simpler case: We need to care about being trim and healthy—more than stuffing our face.

❖ ❖ ❖

IMAGINE our measure of needing to lose weight was: More than an inch—if we could pinch!

❖ ❖ ❖

NO coat, short sleeves, it means it is spring; and time to flourish and succeed at getting trim.

TO best take care of and get thin: Truly love the body you are in.

❖ ❖ ❖

TO lose weight we only need to gain self-control, as in self-check; and if necessary, from time to time, self-correct.

❖ ❖ ❖

WHEN doing what we like has gotten us into the unhealthy and obese state that we are in; we need to do what we do not like, in order to get into a shape, healthy and thin.

❖ ❖ ❖

WHEN we start losing weight, that frown; also, will into a smile, turn around.

❖ ❖ ❖

WHEN your belly keeps expanding like it not should, it is more than ok to be hungry—it is something good.

LOSS

LOSS can be great, like of—pride or prejudice or weight.

❖ ❖ ❖

LOSS can bring us more together.

❖ ❖ ❖

MAY it not darken your heart, and may it be brief; may you gain insight and wisdom and understanding from your—loss and woe and grief.

❖ ❖ ❖

SO often on the morrow, softened will be your sorrow.

❖ ❖ ❖

WHEN we do not have, we have something to strive for.

LOVE

IT is not means or money that makes the difference that will set our life apart, but simply whether we have love in our heart.

❖ ❖ ❖

IT shows the deepest sagacity and soundest smarts, when we make decisions—with love in our hearts.

❖ ❖ ❖

LIVE simply, but love lavishly.

❖ ❖ ❖

LOVE does not love now and then, love does not turn its back and walk away; love loves beyond the very end, love with you will always stay.

❖ ❖ ❖

LOVE in your hand and heart and eye, is as powerful as the sun in the summer's sky.

THE best place to be: Is where there is—only you and me.

❖   ❖   ❖

WE all have, all the while we live: All our love—yet to give.

❖   ❖   ❖

WHEN you value love above anything, know that you have everything.

MAKING IT THROUGH

ALWAYS it is what we choose to do, that will be what sees us through.

❖ ❖ ❖

BEFORE it happens we may think "what would I do?" But if the unfortunate happens, we will afterward find, somehow—we made it through.

❖ ❖ ❖

DUE to our diverse abilities stemming from our creation: We will make it through better, by working together, every—person and culture and nation.

❖ ❖ ❖

IF I had to sum up this part of my philosophy, I would say; it is entirely very simple, and all about: Making it—anyway.

IT does not matter if you fall, and poise and grace and elegance matters least of all; what is important is that you make it through, even if on your stomach—you have to crawl.

❖   ❖   ❖

IT was malice and vindictiveness and spite, what they decided to do; but know that it despite, you can—still, make it through.

❖   ❖   ❖

REGARDLESS of what comes your way, know that—you will always be ok.

❖   ❖   ❖

THEY tried to slow and block and stop you, but it is fine and good and gay; because you will always make it in this world—anyway.

MAKING IT THROUGH (cont.)

THOSE that are genuinely appreciative of what others for them do; people are usually happy to help them, try and make it through.

❖ ❖ ❖

WHEN it has reached the too-little-too-late point for us, may we learn from what we did not do; and rather than fretting and regretting, help the next person—to make it through.

❖ ❖ ❖

WHEN most of the time you do what you can do, it will most likely be all that is needed for you to make it through.

❖ ❖ ❖

WHEN you are reeling from life's blows, because this is how often it goes, remember there is still much you can do: Get on your belly or hands and knees two; stay low and know, you can—drag yourself past and through.

WHEN you cannot make it through standing tall, then on your hands and knees—claw and crawl.

❖   ❖   ❖

WHILE we need to work hard to make it through day after day; we also sometimes, need something—to go our way.

❖   ❖   ❖

WITH intentions that are pure and good and true, it cannot be other than—you make it through.

❖   ❖   ❖

YOU are going in strong and brave and bright, and will emerge stronger and braver and brighter—than you ever thought you might!

YOU are in the deepest depths of low, but still, baby, know; that you need to be grateful and God praise, for when it is time your burden will be raised; and profound peace and power and grandeur will be who are you, all because—you came through.

❖ ❖ ❖

YOU are young and smart and good, so in everything you put your mind to; it is a certainty that how could, you but—make it through.

❖ ❖ ❖

YOU have been knocked to the ground, and are seeing stars all around; but still, the outcome is up to you: For there is no need to stand, in order to— pull and scrape and squeeze yourself through.

❖ ❖ ❖

YOU will make it fine, you will make it through; because, quite frankly: You have far too many things here—yet to do.

MATERIAL

FIX what you have, and you will find what you have been searching for.

❖ ❖ ❖

HAVING everything has nothing to do with having things.

❖ ❖ ❖

MORE important than fixing it up to sell, is fixing it up to keep.

❖ ❖ ❖

OUR joy and happiness need not be tied to whether we are old or twenty, whether we are in want or have of everything plenty.

❖ ❖ ❖

REPAIR what you have, and it will be custom made for you; and therefore, better than anything that you can buy new.

TRUE riches we do not reach for with our hands, but hold in our hearts.

❖   ❖   ❖

WE are far better off having more than we show, than showing more than we have.

❖   ❖   ❖

WE may not have the best, but it is the best that we have.

❖   ❖   ❖

YOU need no thing else.

MENTAL HEALTH

BECOMING healthier in our mind, leads to healthier choices of every kind.

❖ ❖ ❖

HAVE you had the good fortune of one, who has seen the ruby throat of the humming bird shining in the sun? If so, then you know, that this tiny bird can impart, great well-being by lifting a—heavy-as-a-stone heart.

❖ ❖ ❖

OFTENTIMES, having something that we have to do, is all that is needed to get us depression through.

❖ ❖ ❖

THAT inconsequential event or those hurtful words from decades ago, that we like to in our heads replay; it is an avoidance mechanism, you know, in order to—not do what we need to do, today.

MONEY

ALWAYS being broke never has to leave us broken.

❖   ❖   ❖

DO it and save it, when to make money is the time; because when we need it, we are not guaranteed—to earn a dime.

❖   ❖   ❖

IF you happen to come into money, spend it like you—had not gotten any.

❖   ❖   ❖

IF you have little money, may it matter not a lot; if you have much money, may it also matter not.

❖   ❖   ❖

THE poorest person has more than the richest can buy, when the latter does not possess the love and peace and contentment that can be seen in the former's eye.

THE sum of your wealth is: What you have left after you minus—all your money and everything you own.

❖　❖　❖

WE are far better off having no money and being dirt poor, or earning very little trying to make a living by scrubbing floors, than being rich and powerful from being—bought or silenced or whores.

❖　❖　❖

WHATEVER you make, you can make do.

MOON

KNOW that your friends are never far, when out is the moon and a star.

❖ ❖ ❖

MOTHER Moon comes at our window to peep, at us as we soundly sleep; to make sure that we are ok, then slowly moves along her way.

❖ ❖ ❖

WHEN the night draws near, in a silver dress does she silently appear; the moon, our shining, constant friend, so dear; in order to guide and comfort and assure us—to never fear.

NATURE

GO outdoors, and your troubles will go, you will see; for Nature will come and take them, and at peace you will be.

❖   ❖   ❖

IN Nature, "common" does not mean not beautiful.

❖   ❖   ❖

JUST give a listen on one of your next walks, and you will hear that Nature sings and laughs and whistles as she talks.

❖   ❖   ❖

LIKE of old, let Nature's energy recharge your soul.

❖   ❖   ❖

ON the clouds in the sky, the wind writes Nature's lullaby.

THE stars that shine, are all yours and mine.

❖   ❖   ❖

WE can all experience pure pleasure like a child, from the simplest of things in the wild.

❖   ❖   ❖

WE have only to look up at the clouds moving across the sky, to know that the exalted and glorious and magnificent—is always nearby.

PAIN

HE has an easy smile and never a cry, and is always willing to try; he is the one with the best attitude, but is lucky to be alive; because he was run over by a tractor, it ran all up and down his side. He is in the worst chronic pain, yet every moment of every day, grateful not to be in his grave; and now, he leads the way, as an example to us all in how—to on this earth behave.

❖ ❖ ❖

KNOW that after the temporary pain, strength and fortitude will forever be your gain.

❖ ❖ ❖

OFTEN in this world, no one cares to say this much, too; so first and foremost: I am sorry that this happened to you.

❖ ❖ ❖

SHE is in pain all day and night and all the while, yet always has ready—a little joke to make you smile.

PAIN (cont.)

THOUGH there is travesty, what lessons can we learn from the pain? Let us be brave and humble enough to ask, so that our loss—did not occur in vain.

❖　❖　❖

WE are best qualified, because of our bad experience, and so can take our pain; and turn it into something good, if not for us—for someone else's gain.

❖　❖　❖

YOU have taken many a hit and clouts and punches, that have caused you much pain; but though you have been pounded, you will surely—stand strong on your feet again.

PARENTS

IN the simple act of letting someone know that he or she is heard and understood, we extend the kind of love—that a mother give would.

❖ ❖ ❖

WHAT kind of thing does a good father whisper to a son, while on his knee and still just a little one?: My feelings I don't like to show, but I love you son, know; I want far better than I had, for you my precious lad; choose well what you will a living at make, and what woman you will for a wife take; and may you one day, though I have long been in my grave, remember it was me who—taught you how to shave.

❖ ❖ ❖

YOU need to rest easy, come that future yet inevitable day; be at peace, and know that: When you are gone—your children will be ok.

PREPAREDNESS

ANYTHING can happen at anytime—that changes everything.

❖   ❖   ❖

CAUTION and attention and warning and en garde!: For we may look back and realize we lost paradise, i.e., our environment and home and little yard; call me paranoid or crazy or anything instead, than it to come to pass what I detect; for the unthinkable devastation of nuclear war is likely ahead, thus we all need to—ourselves prepare and protect.

❖   ❖   ❖

IF for health, disease prevention is better than early detection; then for safety, precaution is better than protection.

❖   ❖   ❖

IF in good times we prepare for bad, we can make the bad times better.

IF times are hard, it means we need to plan for harder times.

❖   ❖   ❖

IT is not at all hard to do, so let us take a moment and think it through.

❖   ❖   ❖

LET us prepare for bad times, when times are good; like in the summer's sun, collecting and chopping wood.

❖   ❖   ❖

NATURE is the world's most powerful force, so to prepare properly we need to—entoughen and enstrengthen and reinforce.

❖   ❖   ❖

90% of predicaments, can be predicted.

REGARDLESS of what the disaster is—so long as Nature is well and alive—we will be able to rebuild and enstrengthen and survive.

❖ ❖ ❖

WE are subject to an already supernatural energy and strength and might, yet this divine power we have grievously disturbed; thus, it is not at all hard to surmise: With us Nature is now sorely perturbed, and that this is—anything but wise.

❖ ❖ ❖

WE have been forewarned, so let us select: To fore-plan and fore-prepare and fore-protect.

❖ ❖ ❖

WHEN another cares enough to us alert, we are more equipped to the problem avert.

WHEN the you-know-what hits the fan, you want to have your you-know-what together.

❖ ❖ ❖

WHETHER it is about our health or personal safety or national security, we need to: Over-prepare, in fact, in order to have protection that is the minimum bare.

PRESENCE

FOR a more fulfilling and enriching and rewarding life for you, simply give your full attention—to everything you do.

❖ ❖ ❖

MAY the best thing in life for me and you, be to spend time together, us four or three or two; sitting and talking or walking, nothing fancy or new; but being fully present, and having nothing we need to do.

❖ ❖ ❖

THE best present of all, is simply—your presence above all.

❖ ❖ ❖

THE presence of you, is the present that has the greatest value.

❖ ❖ ❖

TO anyone the best present for us to give, is our undivided presence while we live.

WHEN we are present, we have everything present before us.

❖   ❖   ❖

WHERE we are physically, is where we need to be mentally.

PROBLEMS

ANY problem you can solve, by digging in with your resolve.

❖ ❖ ❖

BE thankful for the woe, for from it you will stronger grow.

❖ ❖ ❖

BUCK up and double down and hold fast, for trial and trouble and tribulation—will not last.

❖ ❖ ❖

IF misfortune must materialize, may our fortune be that it happens to what is material.

❖ ❖ ❖

IN order to be in the clear, before we relax around the fireplace in warmth and comfort and good cheer; before we get the embers glowing and have no smoke, we may first have to—cough and tear and choke.

IN the midst of your troubles I know it is hard to see; but in the end it will have guided you best to—what to do and who you need to be.

❖   ❖   ❖

SURE, it chips and abrades and erodes us, but those rough edges we did not need anyway; difficulty has made us beautiful, like a smooth stream stone, water washes over each day; and what used to make us depressed, not ago very long; now shines and refines, and has made us— unbreakably solid and strong.

❖   ❖   ❖

THE things we cannot do anything about, is not what it is about.

❖   ❖   ❖

THOUGH the problem is complex, the solution may be simple.

PROBLEMS (cont.)

WHAT is most important so that we are empowered moving forward, why it happened perhaps: Is that we get the message from our little—stumbles and accidents and mishaps.

❖ ❖ ❖

WHEN faced with a sad matter, know that in a single moment the face of the matter can change.

❖ ❖ ❖

WHEN it is a problem you admit, you are on the road to fixing it.

❖ ❖ ❖

WHEN set-backs come our way, let us curse not; but say "thank you," for it only seems to be our unlucky lot.

❖ ❖ ❖

WOULD that on a day sunny and warm and swell: That we could not—also catch hell.

QUITTING

BY drawing on your hard and tough and stony grit, it becomes easy—to never quit.

❖　❖　❖

EVEN being bitter, is better than being a quitter.

❖　❖　❖

GIVING up is for the weak, because it is always the easiest thing to do; know that deep within yourself is all the strength you need to—pull yourself up and through.

❖　❖　❖

IF you give up, it is all up.

❖　❖　❖

IT is because of that time, now long ago and away very far; that you had not been a quitter, that today—you are shining like a star.

QUITTING (cont.)

IT is never the time to give up and wail, regardless of how many times we have tried and failed.

❖ ❖ ❖

IT is tough, I know, and you are about to give in; but at it all, instead—laugh and joke and grin.

❖ ❖ ❖

LET us quit quitting and try trying.

❖ ❖ ❖

MANY tried and tried, but failed and failed, so no one blamed them that they gave up and in; but they did not understand what it is all about: It is never—about the win.

❖ ❖ ❖

NEVER say "I cannot" you should; say "I think I can," and soon you will be saying—"I knew I could!"

NO number of reasons can justify our reason to quit, for far always goes even a little—sass and spunk and spirit.

❖ ❖ ❖

SOME before they try, drop out or in cave, for they think it is to no avail; to others no one will bat an eye, since they only gave, up after the loss or fail; but the ones that refuse to quit, why—win and triumph they'll.

❖ ❖ ❖

THOUGH nothing seems to help, never throw in the towel you; because the ones that choose to persevere—are who make it through.

❖ ❖ ❖

TOO young and a whippersnapper and just a pup, you are to even think about—giving up.

YOU can sit and cry and lick your wounds in here, or you can—get back out there!

❖ ❖ ❖

YOU did not come from way down, and back there: To give up now—here.

❖ ❖ ❖

YOU had lost at the game all your life, but it was because you had been a quitter; but now you are a trier, which means inevitably—a winner.

❖ ❖ ❖

YOU have thrown in the towel, there is no hope you believe; but hope will bloom as soon as—that towel you retrieve.

READING

A chapter a day, helps keep the dementia away.

❖ ❖ ❖

NOT everything need have measureable utility, for where would our lives be without a bit of poetry.

❖ ❖ ❖

PICKING up a book, can pick you up.

❖ ❖ ❖

SEPTEMBER always seems to have a way, she knows best how to make on Earth the perfect day; Heaven is then created by—reading a novel and slipping away.

RECOVERY

BEFORE too long, you will be again strong.

❖   ❖   ❖

I am so sorry to say, but no one, in fact, can make it go away; and though you have no one to hold your hand through the night; alone you will make it through, but now your job to do, is to—fight, baby, fight!

❖   ❖   ❖

IT is better to not have to go to the dentist, sure; but when there is a problem, let us be grateful getting patched up is in store.

❖   ❖   ❖

OFTEN, to simply get out of bed, is the first step in feeling better instead.

❖   ❖   ❖

ON the road to recovery is a good route to be on, indeed; and remember, where we are in our path is—where to be we need.

THEY all said it was going to tear you down, reduce you to rubble, and just a shell; but now that you are through it: Nothing has built you up more—robust and hearty and well.

❖   ❖   ❖

THOUGH you are still symptomatic, all the time you are getting better at it.

❖   ❖   ❖

THOUGH you are still weak, each day all along, you are getting more—stout and sturdy and strong.

❖   ❖   ❖

WE need not on ways to attain, more gold or stocks or monetary wealth; but to focus on a regain, of our own precious, priceless health.

❖   ❖   ❖

WOULD that my words would work like a magic spell: May you quickly recover, and in your future—be always well.

RECOVERY (cont.)

YOU were in a deathly state, then and there; but are now healed and healthy and—here.

❖   ❖   ❖

YOUR recovery is bound to be a deliverance, from where you will go on and do all with—renewed purpose and gratitude and exuberance.

RENEWAL

AGAIN your time—will come to shine.

❖ ❖ ❖

FOR a complete renewal, tap into your spiritual fuel.

❖ ❖ ❖

IT is time now to forget the thirst and hunger, pain and poverty, and want and woe; that for many bitter days we have come all too well to know; the years yet to come will truly be the best, where we will find: love and Nature, and peace and quiet and rest.

❖ ❖ ❖

OUR regret and sorrow and darkness, it is time to let pass on; and with hope and joy and love, let us greet the dawn.

THOUGH they may fall on us ever so fast at times, let us treat our problems like summer rain; then like water off a duck's back they will roll off, and the sun will dry our tears and warm us, again.

❖   ❖   ❖

WE had made a bad choice, we had lost our way; but we must let it go in order to: Live the purpose of our lives, today.

❖   ❖   ❖

YOU have much more than merely survived, you are now—refreshed and restored and revived.

RESILIENCE

AFTER the storm when a rainbow comes out, know that it is to say: To you, that despite what has happened—all will be ok.

❖ ❖ ❖

BEAR the punches and the beating rain, take the thrashing and do not complain; believe it or not, it is all fine and good and ok; because more powerful beyond belief, you will—come back the next day.

❖ ❖ ❖

IF need be: Keep quiet and lay low, but always—forward you go.

❖ ❖ ❖

IN spite of it all, you will surely stand tall.

❖ ❖ ❖

IT took all their energy to push and pull and keep you down; but little that they knew then that: You will never—stay long on the ground.

IT wants to throw you to-and-fro, and will not stop until on the floor you go; yet you can always crawl back up, and brace yourself for—the next blow.

❖　❖　❖

KNOW that inside, resilience resides.

❖　❖　❖

LET the storms fall from you like water off a duck's back; and moreover, though they are being pounded—you never hear a quack.

❖　❖　❖

LIKE the tree limb bend, but when even more you have to take; know that: You will make it through and mend—after the break.

❖　❖　❖

MOST of success is not due to chance or good fortune or brilliance; but instead, a result of someone—who chose resilience.

REGARDLESS of what they try to do, they cannot stop the sun from shining on you.

❖   ❖   ❖

THE best way to make it in this life, so full of strife, is simply to: Stay strong, and soldier on.

❖   ❖   ❖

THE will and power within us is nothing to be with toyed; how we can be dispirited and devastated and defeated—yet not destroyed.

❖   ❖   ❖

THEY never had much good to say about you, no; but nevertheless, you will make it in this world—know.

❖   ❖   ❖

THOUGH nobody cares much anymore to give her the time of day; we can take inspiration from Nature, for she always knows how to—find a way.

WHEN even directed toward us, we must endeavor; because of their malicious acts, to put ourselves out never.

❖ ❖ ❖

WHERE today is the sun? My, how stormy it has become. Yes, we can rush in before the rain, so long as we, always tomorrow—come out, again.

❖ ❖ ❖

YOU can take it, baby, about it make no mistake; because baby—you were built to break.

❖ ❖ ❖

YOU have been cuffed in the gut, and in the dirt your face has been ground; yet you are on your feet again, because no amount of clouts and kicks are—ever going to keep you down.

RESILIENCE (cont.)

YOU have been lashed and thrashed and mashed, but it is still going to be ok; because you have now through it all lived, to see, to start with, this day.

❖　❖　❖

YOU have hewn hard, only to find it tough all the way with little respite; but with each swing and stroke, you are empowering yourself—it all despite.

SEASONS

AUTUMN'S riches and abundance and plenty, may be had by all and everyone and any.

❖ ❖ ❖

ESPECIALLY sent from Heaven our way, is each and every summer's day.

❖ ❖ ❖

EVERY season—even winter, at times—has its beauty.

❖ ❖ ❖

ONE'S favorite stage may be no season at all; but a month like August, when summer turns to fall.

❖ ❖ ❖

THE best time for richness is fall: deep colors, warm stews, and luxury fibers and thick fabrics, most of all.

THERE is nothing like spring to in you revive:
The love and thrill and glory of—just being alive.

❖   ❖   ❖

TO autumn added a gentle breeze, and what a joy
it is to watch the trees, of laughing and swinging
and dancing—red and gold and orange leaves.

❖   ❖   ❖

TO witness Nature in spring, may we cannot help
but be: Grateful beyond words to—simply have
eyes that see.

SELF-AWARE

ANYTHING that weighs us down or keeps us in the dark or holds us prisoner, we need to release and let go; to be light and free and able to rise and flourish and flower, and have our pure energy flow.

❖ ❖ ❖

AWARENESS is one short step away from empowerment.

❖ ❖ ❖

BECOMING conscious and self-aware and yourself knowing, are the first steps for self-development and self-growing.

❖ ❖ ❖

BEFORE we can do the hard work, the wear and tear; of improving, we need to become self-aware.

LET us be open to what we do not want about ourselves to know; because from this will spring what we most need to learn in order to improve and grow.

❖   ❖   ❖

NEVER confuse being self-conscious with being self-aware: Of self-consciousness let us let go, of being conscious of ourselves let us embrace in order to better know.

❖   ❖   ❖

THOSE conscious of the larger consciousness make conscious decisions.

❖   ❖   ❖

WE either want to understand what we need for self-improvement or we do not, either way—we choose our lot.

SELF-RELIANT

ALL those times you thought someone would help, and pleaded and waited, but no one came; it made you into someone who today can stand on your own, one—who overcame.

❖　❖　❖

BE em-powered to be me-powered.

❖　❖　❖

BE selfish: Self-made and self-reliant and self-aware, and about self-education and self-discipline care.

❖　❖　❖

BEING self-reliant does not mean being stolid and suffering through; it is about trying to be smart and finding the solutions—from within you.

❖　❖　❖

I know, never alone did you have to face such challenges; but know, on your own you will be the one who manages.

I know, you asked and begged and implored, yet no one cared to help, but that is ok; because you will not only make it anyway, you will make it—better this way.

❖   ❖   ❖

IN art and science and literature, the deck was stacked against them, Darwin and Dickens and Van Gogh; but they made it anyway by: Teaching themselves—what they needed to know.

❖   ❖   ❖

IN self-reliance, indeed, one lesson: Is to rely on your—Smith & Wesson.

❖   ❖   ❖

IN your lowest moments you were left all alone; so certainly by now, you know how to—make it on your own.

IT is best if we are as self-reliant as we can be, that means not being dependent on even something as basic as electricity.

❖ ❖ ❖

IT is not bad if no one helps me and you, but it is not good if we expected them to.

❖ ❖ ❖

IT is when nobody else believes in you, that you most need to believe in yourself.

❖ ❖ ❖

NATURE does not suffer the helpless gladly.

❖ ❖ ❖

REGARDLESS of what is to be: You will always have thee.

THE best possible course, is to be an individual of resource.

❖   ❖   ❖

THE more capable and competent you are, the more able to help others by far.

❖   ❖   ❖

THE more empowered, the more self-reliant; the more self-reliant, the more empowered.

❖   ❖   ❖

THE more self-reliant are we, the more others can rely on you and me.

❖   ❖   ❖

THE more self-reliant are you, the more you can for another do.

THE more you are now able to rely on yourself, the less in the future you will have to depend on anyone else.

❖ ❖ ❖

THE way to be self-reliant is when you are in need of help: First and second and third—look to yourself.

❖ ❖ ❖

THOSE of us that have been given zilch and nothing and neigh; will always in this world, be able to—on ourselves rely.

❖ ❖ ❖

THOUGH today each step you have to carve out on your own, in the future you will look back in amazement at how much you have grown.

SELF-RELIANT (cont.)

THOUGH you were never blessed, never loved, given no legacy, and not a penny for sure; not only have you now got in your head brains, but: spirit in your step, will in your muscles, and strong blood in your veins.

❖　❖　❖

TO forever, as you go through life, stay young and vibrant and thriving inside: Keep your good nature and positive attitude and curiosity as— constant companions at your side.

❖　❖　❖

WHAT was owed you, what was due you, what should have been yours—you never got; yet by your own grit and sweat and toil, greater rewards one day will—be possible not.

❖　❖　❖

WHEN no one will help you, to help yourself you are forced; but from it your self-power and independence and competency will surely be reinforced.

WHEN you do not lean on anyone else, understand; that taller and stronger and straighter—you grow and stand.

❖ ❖ ❖

WHEN you think you have no one, know that you always have yourself.

❖ ❖ ❖

WITHIN you is indeed: All that you will ever need.

❖ ❖ ❖

YOU know that you are self-reliant when there is no one that can do anything for you, that you cannot do for yourself.

SERVICE

BE it our good fortune or this beautiful day, it is not because we it deserve; we are given it because we have all been—chosen to serve.

❖　❖　❖

DESPITE how fine, ultimately it will matter not any award or medal or trophy that we have won; but the bigger-picture view, that is, our duty—we need to have done.

❖　❖　❖

FOR value untold, serve your soul.

❖　❖　❖

IN order to the best of ourselves to the world give, a life of service let us choose to live.

❖　❖　❖

THE greatest deed that we can do, is when we are of help or aid or use or value.

THE reason it is important to get our lives in order, is so to the world we have something better to offer.

❖   ❖   ❖

TRUE service is performed with nothing for you—no payment or prize or reward—for what you do.

❖   ❖   ❖

WHEN our occupation is one of service, our wages are never ending bliss.

❖   ❖   ❖

YOU will never go amiss, if you live a life of service.

SICKNESS

CAREFUL: When the symptoms now we dismiss, the cure later—we may miss.

❖   ❖   ❖

LET us understand the reason for, and get the message from our health scare; it is not conducting business as usual for, but of ourselves to—take better care.

❖   ❖   ❖

THE last thing a patient needs to do, is to have to—fight the doctors too.

❖   ❖   ❖

THOUGH it is a heavy load and weight and burden, forge on through your symptoms, and yourself steel; for this period is what is most needed, in order for you to heal.

WE can get sick of fighting, and that is when we are perfectly well; imagine what can happen then, to those not feeling so swell.

❖   ❖   ❖

WHEN we are hurting and are in pain because we are so ill; may we have love and kindness and encouragement—and the better health they instill.

❖   ❖   ❖

WHICHEVER way we can, somehow in our duress: Let us seek to find the present in the gift of illness.

SIMPLICITY

BE a simple woman or man, for there is nothing—purer and truer and better than.

❖ ❖ ❖

CAREFUL: Complicated people end up living complicated lives.

❖ ❖ ❖

MAY our desires be such that we will have all the desires of our heart.

❖ ❖ ❖

MOST of us need not much to be happy, just one or two things to sometimes go our way; and we feel that all is again right with the world, and each, a beautiful day.

❖ ❖ ❖

TO be simple, to love, and to be true, is all that— we ever need to do.

SPIRITUALITY

EVERYTHING is easier with spirituality.

❖ ❖ ❖

IN everything you do, may your soul come through.

❖ ❖ ❖

LET us always seek to be: With the divine in you and me.

❖ ❖ ❖

ONLY under the exact correct conditions like with a certain composition can common carbon crystallize to diamond form; just so, we have all been created and are born, and though on the outside we naturally get weather-worn; inside, with what is light and bright and right—we forever shine and are adorned.

❖ ❖ ❖

THE ones that surely know where they are going, are surely the ones not in the knowing.

THE universe is in fact, in silent and loving and eager expectation waiting to see, to be exact: What we will do, and who we are choosing to be.

❖ ❖ ❖

THERE is great spirituality in attention.

❖ ❖ ❖

THERE is a formidable force unseen, and unexplained here for sure; but its presence can be gleaned, because when we are lost—it hands us an oar.

❖ ❖ ❖

THEY tried, but your body they did not break; they messed with, but your mind they could not take; and due to it all, your spirit has—never been more awake.

❖ ❖ ❖

THOUGH our body has been bowed and broken and breached, our spirit—cannot be reached.

SPIRITUALITY (cont.)

THOUGH your body may a prisoner be, slaving at a job or perhaps even literally, know that—your soul is free.

❖   ❖   ❖

WE can sense that we are not alone, so have no fear; for there is indeed something largely unknown, and invisible here; a loving presence or all-knowing consciousness that guides us and is— always near.

❖   ❖   ❖

WE may be broken in body because we exceeded our limit, but our soul is: free and whole and boundless and infinite.

❖   ❖   ❖

WHEN we lose in this world materially, our net profit is higher if we then choose to gain spiritually.

STRENGTH

A torrential storm with winds that howl and whip and blow; that it is best if we are strong and hardy, it comes to us show.

❖　❖　❖

BEAR and brace and brave it through, stay stout and solid and soldier on you!

❖　❖　❖

ENDLESS difficulty always for you, but turn it around is what you must do; because this is why you are going it through: To make you strong— like you never knew.

❖　❖　❖

IN the past, when all were surprised by your strength, even you did not know then I bet: That baby, ain't nobody—had seen nothing yet!

STRENGTH (cont.)

IT is the weak and the bad and the cowardly, that waffle and waiver to and fro; for the strong and the good and the brave—our "yes" means yes, and our "no" means no.

❖ ❖ ❖

KEEP it foremost in your knowing: That you have not lived this long, without growing—tough and staunch and strong.

❖ ❖ ❖

SOME people give us strength, just from being who they are.

❖ ❖ ❖

THE more they push and pull you down: The stronger you get from—picking yourself off the ground.

❖ ❖ ❖

THE strength you see in one way today, will manifest in another manner on another day.

WE can all whine and wallow and cry, over how they did us wrong; but one day we will no longer ask why, when we find from it we have grown—smart and stalwart and strong.

❖   ❖   ❖

WE have had tears and sadness and mourning at length; now let us take joy in what is good, and this will be our strength.

❖   ❖   ❖

WHAT matters is not the number of medals on our chest; but what it is made of, the quality of the mettle in our breast.

❖   ❖   ❖

WHEN you tangle with the devil and win, invincible strength is gained as you—overcome sin.

YOU used to be weak, but now you have will and spirit and are strong; enstrengthened you were by being meek, and now few—can stand as long.

❖　❖　❖

YOU used to cry, but now you hold your head up high; you used to not know, but how from it all you did grow; there were times you could not hold on, but now you go for the brass ring—hard and sure and strong.

STRIVING

ALL clear, does not produce a beautiful sunset; but add some clouds, and it becomes the best yet; so it is with adversity in our lives, from it we gain strength—from knowing what it is to strive.

❖ ❖ ❖

LET us make it a plan, to always do what we can.

❖ ❖ ❖

THERE is so much more we accomplish could, if only we strive would.

❖ ❖ ❖

THOUGH most days have been about just surviving, immeasurable strength you have gained all along from your striving; which now fortifies your life as—enriched and rewarding and thriving.

THOUGH subject to unfairness from the word go, you can smile inwardly to yourself because you know: That you will make it better than the rest, and shine like the sun among the best; because the more strength you will derive—the more you have to strive.

❖　❖　❖

YOU never caught a break, and always had the toughest row to hoe; but you never whined or complained, and will succeed, you just know; plus even more you will have gained, because you will have your—strength from striving—to show.

❖　❖　❖

YOU thriving, is who you always wanted to be—toward striving.

STRUGGLING

BE it may, that we have in order to play, when it is getting just too hard—another card.

❖　❖　❖

FROM trying you are weary, and now weak from the fight; but never give in and indulge in the teary, though you have no energy left, no might; the way out, is to stay sure and stout and do not shout; for submitted for you to do, is to limp or drag or pull, but—get yourself through.

❖　❖　❖

IT is not the quarter-mile cake walk that makes us strong; but the yard that we have to axe and saw and drill through, every inch of the way, all along.

❖　❖　❖

IT is weary and woeful and worrisome, but know it, that you will gain; and have to show for it, insight and wisdom and strength—from the strain.

STRUGGLING (cont.)

IT was an invisible hand that helped you back up, all those times that you had fallen; thus, each obstacle guides us closer to finding the higher purpose of our life—our calling.

❖ ❖ ❖

NOW you have everything and can do anything, and it is all because—you started with nothing.

❖ ❖ ❖

US knowing our destiny, does not come automatically; that we will have to struggle to fulfill it, is a necessity.

❖ ❖ ❖

WHEN we are in the middle of our despair, we do not know it, but I have seen it again and again; somehow, as long as we keep going, it works out—for the best in the end.

WHEN you can no longer take the pounding, it is fine if you fall; so long as you keep going, be it on your belly—you have to crawl.

❖ ❖ ❖

WHEN you cannot accomplish it with ease or grace or in any way complete, get through by hanging on—by the skin of your teeth.

❖ ❖ ❖

WHEN you have struggled for what you have earned, and have had to even fight to what was yours keep; you know how to survive and bounce back and—land on your feet!

❖ ❖ ❖

YOU are old and tired and haggard, and now more bones than meat; it means you have to strain, but struggle to your feet; or on your hands and knees crawl, if that is too great a feat; but toil through your next step, and even if broken, in the end—you will not be beat.

STRUGGLING (cont.)

YOU are up to your neck in mud, struggling, it is what life is all about; yet you will emerge clean and spick-and-span, because your heart is— resolute and valiant and stout.

❖   ❖   ❖

YOUR path is hard-baked, rock-strewn, and the slope, slick and steep; but never forget: What we sow, we reap; therefore, not only will make it you, but more—true and pure and solidly too.

SUCCESS

IN your ultimate success you must believe, never give up and it you will achieve.

❖ ❖ ❖

IT leads to success and is simple, yet of it few know: Simply being someone that says "yes"— instead of "no."

❖ ❖ ❖

KEEP trying hard, until the game is done; play your last card, until you are left with none; keep fighting, after all hope is gone; for this is the way that—true success is won.

❖ ❖ ❖

MAY all be very well with you, and in everything you choose to do—happiness and fulfillment and success too.

NO matter how many times they win at beating you down, a success of yourself you make when you pull yourself back up—for another round.

❖ ❖ ❖

NO one ever told us, I know; how to be a successful woman or man; but those that have come before did us show: The way is by doing—all that we can.

❖ ❖ ❖

SOME spent their energy to push you down, others did not care to lend a hand; yet you always knew, that you would somehow make it through; and now they all look up and marvel, at the success—that has become of you.

❖ ❖ ❖

SUCCESS is never about being rich or famous like a star, but always about the road traveled thusfar.

SUCCESS will come when we do not want the carrot on the stick only, the win; but when we sincerely and altruistically put—something of ourselves in.

❖ ❖ ❖

THE trademark of the successful ones, that accomplish and rise and up go; is that they say "yes" anyway, instead of trying to find reasons to justify a "no".

❖ ❖ ❖

THEY tried to keep you down, certainly they kicked you around; but little did they know, in those moments that they did so: Their failure they secured, and your success—they ensured.

❖ ❖ ❖

TO be a winner in this world in everything you do: Be sure to fear the Lord, and give—the devil his due.

TRUE success is not about where we are, but about how we came—to have reached this far.

❖   ❖   ❖

WEALTH and success beyond measure comes when we are not checking and summing and measuring.

❖   ❖   ❖

WHEN reach the top you, only—over-the-top will do!

❖   ❖   ❖

WITH a persevering attitude and a positive stance, you will be a success—regardless of your circumstance.

❖   ❖   ❖

YOU could not be more of a success if you, in this life get to do: The thing that nothing better— you would want to.

SUCCESS (cont.)

YOU have no training nor contacts nor help, plus there is no money so others from it refrain; but your heart and soul and sweat are in it, so you will be a success, and—able to it sustain.

❖   ❖   ❖

YOU know what you are doing, how to get things done, and how to make it work.

SUICIDE

Dear young man or woman or perhaps boy or girl—you would not contemplate suicide; if you knew of the consciousness from which you came, are part of, and how—you are miraculously alive; for more special than stardust, purer than diamond—you crystallized from; and those that have been on the brink, now cannot believe that— they were so dumb. Immaculate glory will one day be yours for the taking; when you will be so grateful to be alive, you will be—kneeling and bawling and aching!

❖   ❖   ❖

Death is not for you, for you have much work—unknown—yet to do.

❖   ❖   ❖

I know, it is rough, but our duty is to brave it; we need to get more tough, and face the future and not fear it.

IT can only get to be too much trouble to live, when to no one we care to anything give.

❖   ❖   ❖

THE way to always care to live, regardless of our age, or what illness or disease or disability comes along: Is to fortify ourselves with a moral sense that is—good and right and strong.

❖   ❖   ❖

THE way to make it always be worth living, is to something of yourself to others be giving.

❖   ❖   ❖

WE do not have to know why we desire to live, nor do we have to even want to survive; but we need to know that some things are just a must: Like never by your own hand—not being alive.

❖   ❖   ❖

YOU are made of much stronger than that constitution, for suicide to—ever be the solution.

SUN

GREATER beauty and riches than can be told, is present in a sunset of—pink and orange and gold.

❖ ❖ ❖

IN winter it lifts us as if it were spring, any little bit of sun the day does bring.

❖ ❖ ❖

NO one says "Good morning" like the sun.

❖ ❖ ❖

SUCH a common and ordinary thing; yet what, in fact, profound joy it can bring: The sun—simply shining in.

❖ ❖ ❖

THE absolute second it does appear, the sun brings forth—warmth and gladness and cheer.

❖ ❖ ❖

THE sun like as of old, spins grey—into gold.

THE sun makes all the difference in the world.

❖   ❖   ❖

WE can all be like the sun, with nothing to hide: glorious and powerful and yet—no pride.

❖   ❖   ❖

WITH the trees green, and the sky and lake blue, a perfect day is had with just—the sun and you.

THINKING

IF you think you can, of course, you will most likely succeed; if you think that it is impossible, this too, will be the outcome guaranteed.

❖　❖　❖

IT should all be water under the bridge, though; if not, by changing our thinking, we can make it so.

❖　❖　❖

JUST keep thinking and you are sure to, figure out how to make it through.

❖　❖　❖

OFTENTIMES we can better think, when we sit down with pen and paper and ink.

❖　❖　❖

WE can allow all our days on Earth to be a living hell, or we can choose to make them like an enchanted from Heaven spell. \

TODAY

IT was cruel, it was brutal, it was like in your face a pow; but never let your yesterday—ruin your now.

❖　❖　❖

LET us not lose today over a dreaded day that may not come; for if it comes to pass, we will be able to it overcome.

❖　❖　❖

LOOKING at ourselves through the eyes of a child shows best what we need for distinguishment; it is not money or status or power that was meant, but—bringing love and being engaged and present.

❖　❖　❖

TODAY is ta-da!

❖　❖　❖

WHEN we treasure not a present, but the present, our time will always be well spent.

WHEN we worry about tomorrow today, every second we are throwing away.

❖   ❖   ❖

WOULD that we would not have to have the time far past; before these soon to be long ago moments, we appreciate at last.

TOUGHNESS

GROWING up you had it rough, and you did what you needed to stay alive; but it has created a you, hard and tough, someone that will always— know how to survive.

❖　❖　❖

LIFE may be smooth, but most likely it will be rough; prepare for all that may come your way, and that means—learning how to be tough.

❖　❖　❖

THIS world is as cold and coarse and hard as rock, and as rough; but the scrapes and cuts and bruises teach us fine lessons, in being—thick-skinned and tough.

❖　❖　❖

TO what is impossibly tough today, tomorrow "no sweat" you will say.

WE need to form thicker skin, than to allow bullying—to do us in.

❖ ❖ ❖

WHEN you are about to give up, because you have had quite enough; when the night has been too long, and the road too rough; remember, that it is all to: Grow you up—hardy and powerful and tough.

❖ ❖ ❖

WITH all the aches and pains, aging and disease and disability can be rough; that is why we need to do all we can to get more—solid and sturdy and tough.

❖ ❖ ❖

YOU are black and blue and red, and have had more than enough; but you are made of much tougher than even you know of stuff; so get back up because—you can take another cuff!

TRYING

BECAUSE it is easier for them to do, does not mean that it is impossible for you.

❖　❖　❖

BETWEEN not trying and failure the line, between trying and success—is as fine.

❖　❖　❖

GIVE it your all—then give some more.

❖　❖　❖

IF only we would—we could.

❖　❖　❖

IT is dead easy to give up and cry; we show what we are made of by—how much we try.

❖　❖　❖

IT is when we reach and stretch and give it a try, that we do what we are supposed to, you and I.

LIKE how in fall Nature spreads endless seed, we do not keep trying—and not succeed.

❖   ❖   ❖

SOMEONE like you cannot succeed they all say; but keep trying, and when you look back you will find that—you made it anyway.

❖   ❖   ❖

THEY were wondering, so asked how you made it, and suspected you must have swindled or cheated or lied; but it is an honorable and powerful yet short story, in three words you can tell them— because you tried.

❖   ❖   ❖

WE are sure to improve our lot, if we try until we cannot.

❖   ❖   ❖

WE do not always need to know the reason why, but we need to know we always need to try.

WE should never start crying, because we should never be done trying.

❖ ❖ ❖

WHEN you are too tired, and no longer have the energy, and are on your last try; may willing be: the Fates or the universe or the God in the sky.

❖ ❖ ❖

WHETHER by design or will or perchance, the ones that keep trying always—get another chance.

❖ ❖ ❖

YOU could have tried, they would have said; but that you did not try, now they cannot say instead.

❖ ❖ ❖

YOU did not make it, but how could you have succeeded, no one was on your side; and yet, the world is now a better place—because you tried.

TURNING IT AROUND

ALLOW yourself not to be dragged under when problems come like they are bound; but jump right in, immerse yourself, for when you learn to swim—you have turned it around.

❖ ❖ ❖

BABY I know, but the reason it is happening to you, is because to turn it around is what—you are supposed to do.

❖ ❖ ❖

EVEN though it is not working out like it should, you can still turn it around into something good.

❖ ❖ ❖

I know terrible adversity has come your way; but by what you do, you can top and exceed and surpass all others—anyway.

TURNING IT AROUND (cont.)

I know, you are depressed and disheartened and disillusioned—but you have to keep plugging away; of course you are doing the right thing—you just need to take it day by day; soon you will be basking in the light, and looking back, you would not have—wanted it any other way!

❖ ❖ ❖

IF you are walking the ground, you can turn it around.

❖ ❖ ❖

LET it enable you "another brick in the wall," to climb up and reach the top and stand tall; and so, you will rise until you tower, and all because you chose to—turn your pain into power.

❖ ❖ ❖

LET us pray that we can save it and turn it around: By keeping the spirit of this great country within us—from it going down.

TURNING IT AROUND (cont.)

NEVER have a doubt, though you feel low and down and out, that turning it around is—what it is all about.

❖　❖　❖

STAY where you are, stand your ground; when trial and setbacks and difficulty come your way, never let them pull you down; because the reason it was submitted to you in the first place, is to— turn it around.

❖　❖　❖

SURE, medicine or science or law can explain what happened, but only in a most limited way; for the bigger-picture view, for an understanding that is true, for the ultimate reason it happened to you—listen to what philosophy has to say.

THE generation 80 years and older is the best among us today: Of what they think and their opinions, they are not afraid to say; they have survived, and know best how to make it, due to— the worst having come their way.

❖　❖　❖

THE reason why lemons were given to you, is because to make lemonade is—what you are supposed to do.

❖　❖　❖

THOUGH they never had an encouraging word to you their child to say; and later you received cusses and clouts instead of pay; you never envied the ones mollycoddled day in and out day; for you somehow knew you would do far better than them all in—making in this world, your way.

❖　❖　❖

WE can turn bad into good by taking our hurt and loss and bust, and making it into for someone else, a plus.

WHEN trouble happens we can sit and sulk and cry, or we can make an effort to turn it around—by giving a harder try.

❖   ❖   ❖

YOU can, it is no joke, turn a minus into a plus— with one stroke.

❖   ❖   ❖

YOUR idea or goal or project is simply not working out, and perhaps it was not meant to do, since it cannot get off the ground; but this is precisely what it is all about, because it was in fact, destined for you—to turn it all around.

WHAT WAS MEANT

AS long as we have in our body breath, let us do what we are here to do until death.

❖　❖　❖

AT the time, of course, we would rather not have to struggle, me and you; but in the end, we would have wanted to have done—what was meant for us to do.

❖　❖　❖

IT is too big a job, I understand; it is too overwhelming, but do what you can; you don't think you can finish, I know; but just start from where you are, and forward go; and you doubt it is important or will matter, I fully see; but it is what you must do—to be who you were meant to be.

❖　❖　❖

IT may not be what you want, but it is what you must do: The thing in this life that has been submitted—to you and only you.

WHAT WAS MEANT (cont.)

JUST as the birds sing because they have a song, when we fine-tune our innate abilities what we produce is—pure and sweet and strong.

❖ ❖ ❖

JUST as when we exercise we have to reach and stretch and lift to make our bodies more able; depending on what we do about the difficulties in life, what was intended for us, it will enable.

❖ ❖ ❖

PART of us will always be and has always been; and for the few brief moments we get on this earth to spend; let us make heaven here, for no other is there; by living right and good and true—as we were intended to do.

❖ ❖ ❖

SIMPLY be honest and true, in everything you do, and you will be living the life, that was meant for you.

To find in this world what is your part: What does tell you your heart?

❖   ❖   ❖

WE are all given a chance at life, and certain circumstances handed; we were meant to be the best that we can be, considering what has been gifted and bestowed and granted.

❖   ❖   ❖

WE must do our little part, be it—science or religion or art.

❖   ❖   ❖

WHEN there have been so many roadblocks, and you feel cannot go on you: Take comfort in and draw strength from the fact that—it was meant for you to do.

WHEN we help others in need it helps them, sure; but when it was what we were supposed to do—it helps us even more.

❖ ❖ ❖

WHEN you open your eyes each day, be grateful that you have been granted another say; there is important work yet to do, that in all this world— can only be done by you.

❖ ❖ ❖

YOU will achieve it, you will see: Who it is that—you were meant to be.

WHY ARE WE HERE?

IN order to here give, is the reason we here live.

❖   ❖   ❖

IN this test to see how you act, to see what you do:
Not only pass, but with—flying colors may you!

❖   ❖   ❖

IT is a simple yet profound question: Why are we
here? And the answer is equally so: To see what
we decide to do, and about what we choose to
care.

❖   ❖   ❖

OF the theories, this one explains the evidence
best: As to why we are here, that it is all—a test.

❖   ❖   ❖

SO simple is the purpose of this life that we live:
It is to first survive, then learn and grow—in order
to give.

WHY ARE WE HERE? (cont.)

THE logic for which is anything but clear, since nearly all of life is to struggle and suffer: Why is it we are here? All of life is a test to see: First if— then how—we choose to persevere.

❖ ❖ ❖

THE only way to pass the test, the only way to successfully finish the race, is to: Choose purity and love and toward all others—show grace.

❖ ❖ ❖

THE purpose of life is not to amass wealth on the earth, or show our power or prove our worth; but in whatever way we can: To help another along, as with a kind word or good deed or song.

❖ ❖ ❖

YOU tried and tried but lost, and now are too tired to keep bailing. To help continue going, hold tight in your knowing: It is a test, where the grade matters not, be it passing or failing; but a trial designed specifically for you, and only and just and simply—to see what you would do!

AFTERWORD

I remain—yours sincerely.

❖   ❖   ❖

www.ingramcontent.com/pod-product-compliance
Lightning Source LLC
Chambersburg PA
CBHW021954090426
42811CB00001B/19